ANIMALS IN THE CITY

Cats

Ava Podmorow

Explore other books at:
WWW.ENGAGEBOOKS.COM

VANCOUVER, B.C.

e WWW.ENGAGEBOOKS.COM

Cats: Level Pre-1
Animals in the City
Podmorow, Ava 2004 –
Text © 2022 Engage Books
Design © 2022 Engage Books

Edited by: A.R. Roumanis
and Sarah Harvey

Text set in Epilogue

FIRST EDITION / FIRST PRINTING

LIBRARY AND ARCHIVES CANADA CATALOGUING IN PUBLICATION

Title: Cats / Ava Podmorow.
Names: Podmorow, Ava, author.
Description: Series statement: Animals in the city
Engaging readers: level pre-1, beginner.

Identifiers: Canadiana (print) 2022039640X | Canadiana (ebook) 20220396418
ISBN 978-1-77476-756-6 (hardcover)
ISBN 978-1-77476-757-3 (softcover)
ISBN 978-1-77476-758-0 (epub)
ISBN 978-1-77476-759-7 (pdf)

Subjects:
LCSH: Readers (Elementary)
LCSH: Readers—Cats
LCGFT: Readers (Publications)

Classification: LCC PE1119.2 .P63 2022 | DDC J428.6/2—DC23

This project has been made possible in part
by the Government of Canada.

Canada

Not all cats are
pet cats.

Some city cats do not have homes.

They are called strays.

Stray cats live in cities to stay warm and find food.

Stray cats
often like to
live in groups.

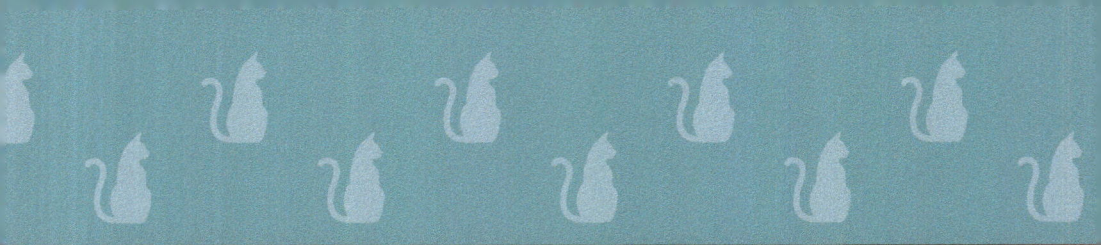

A group of cats is called a clowder.

11

A male cat is called a tom.

A female cat is called a molly or a queen.

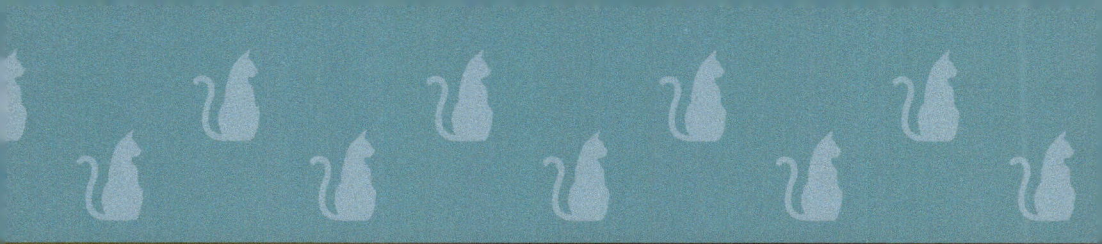

All cats love
to sleep.

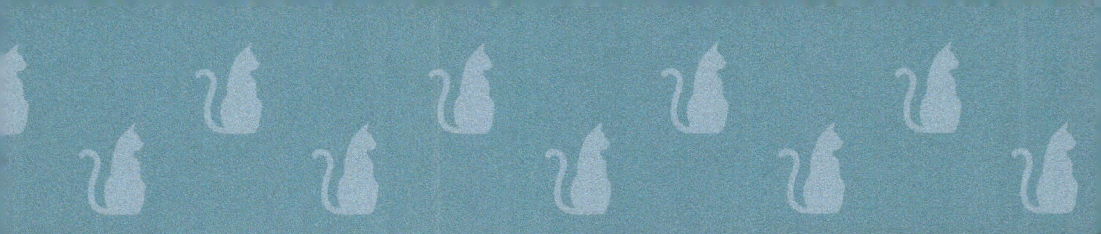

They sleep for about 14 hours each day!

15

A cat's tail can help it balance.

Tail

They have long whiskers and sharp claws.

Whiskers

Claws

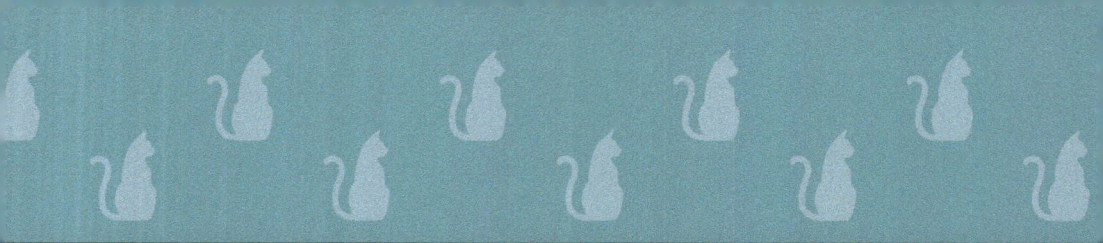

Cats are able to
see really well
at night.

18

They also have a strong sense of smell and a great sense of hearing.

21

Cats like to be clean!

They use their tongue
to lick themselves
and others.

23

Cats can jump more than five times their own height!

24

A cat's whiskers are very important.

They help cats adapt to changes in their space.

Stray cats may be cute but not friendly.

I might scratch if you try and pet me!

Explore other books in the Animals In The City series.

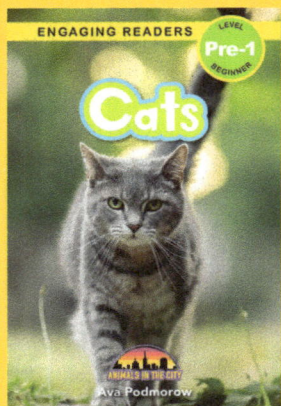

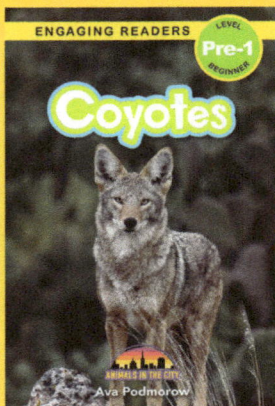

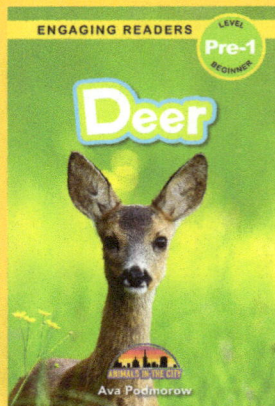

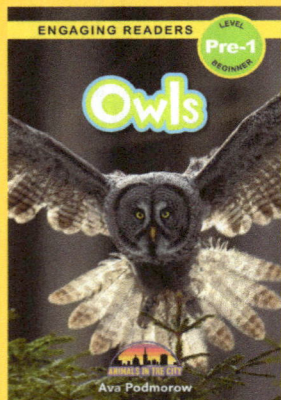

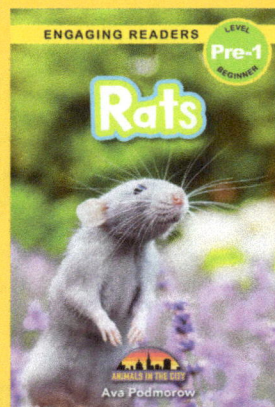

Visit www.engagebooks.com/readers

Explore level 1 readers with the Animals That Make a Difference series.

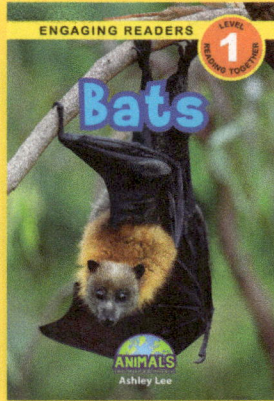

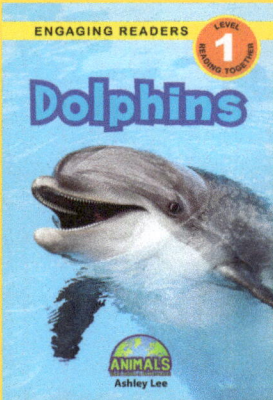

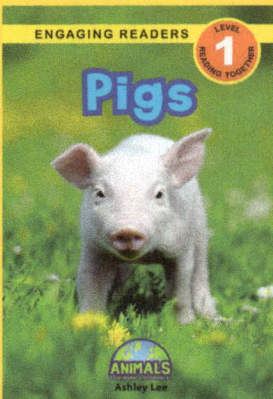

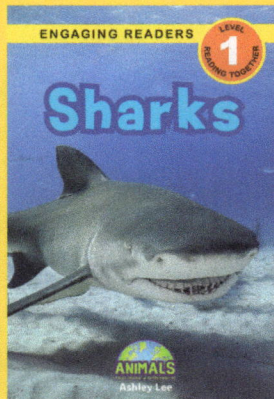

Visit www.engagebooks.com/readers